All Aboard
TRAINS

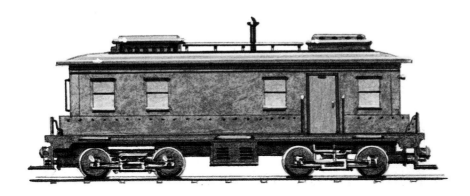

A Grosset & Dunlap **ALL ABOARD BOOK**®

1997 Printing

The illustrations in this book have previously
appeared in *The Big Book of Real Trains*,
published by Grosset & Dunlap.

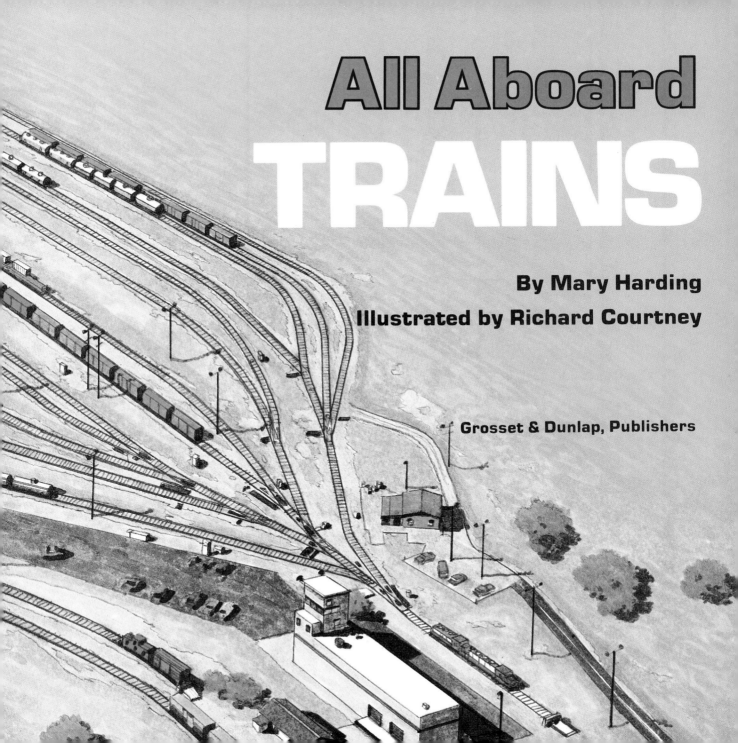

All Aboard
TRAINS

By Mary Harding

Illustrated by Richard Courtney

Grosset & Dunlap, Publishers

Freight Trains

Freight trains haul just about anything—lumber, food, even animals—but they never carry passengers. A diesel-electric locomotive pulls a freight train. The locomotive can have one or more power units. This locomotive has two power units, back to back. When it is hooked up to a train of freight cars, it will be able to haul many tons of cargo.

DIESEL-ELECTRIC LOCOMOTIVE

There are different kinds of freight cars for different kinds of cargo.

Gondola cars are used for heavy cargo. This one carries a load of steel pipes that will be used to build a new office tower.

GONDOLA CAR

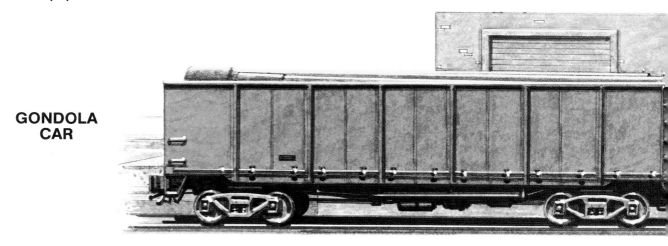

This refrigerator car keeps fresh fruit cool so it will not spoil on the way to the supermarkets in the city.

REFRIGERATOR CAR

This livestock car carries cows on their way to a dairy farm. The openings in the sides allow fresh air in so the cows can breathe.

LIVESTOCK CAR

A boxcar can carry any kind of boxed or packed cargo. This one is being loaded with computers.

BOXCAR

Hopper cars carry loose cargo such as grain or sand. The cargo is poured into the top of the car and unloaded through a chute at the bottom. These hopper cars are being filled with coal. The coal will be delivered to an electric power plant to be used as fuel.

HOPPER CAR

Tank cars transport liquid cargo. This tank car is filled with oil.
The workers are transferring the oil to a tank truck for delivery
to gas stations in a nearby town.

TANK CAR

Flatcars have no top or sides. Their cargo is strapped on with ropes or chains. A piggyback flatcar is extra long. It can carry two huge truck trailers.

PIGGYBACK FLATCAR

Some piggyback flatcars transport heavy shipping containers. This container is filled with a cargo of books bound for a warehouse. A heavy crane lifts the entire container and loads it onto a flatcar. The container will be carried by train halfway across the country.

When the freight train reaches its destination, another crane will lift the container off the flatcar and place it directly onto a flatbed truck for the last stage of the journey.

AUTO-RACK CAR

The auto-rack car is a special flatcar used for transporting new automobiles. It can have two or three levels and carry up to 18 autos.

To unload, the racks are adjusted so that the automobiles can be driven from one auto-rack car to another.

A caboose is the very last car on some freight trains. This is the train crew's home and the conductor's office. From the cupola, or roof look-out, the conductor can check for signals from the crew at the front of the train.

CABOOSE

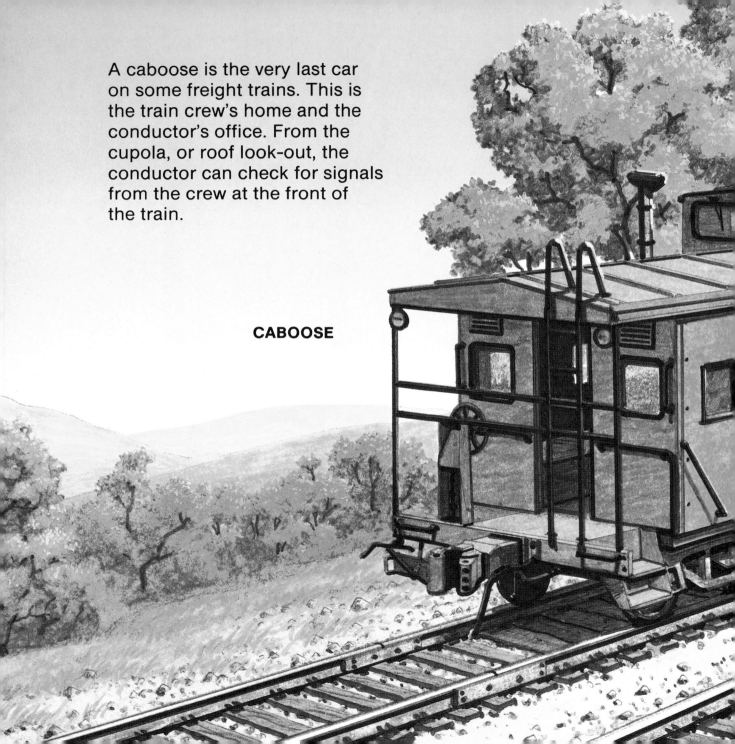

Passenger Trains

Passenger trains carry people and baggage. Some trains travel only from suburbs to the city. These are called commuter trains. Other passenger trains travel across the country. These are called inter-city trains. Many passenger trains are pulled by electric locomotives. Electric locomotives do not produce their own power. They get it from a power plant miles away.

ELECTRIC
LOCOMOTIVE

Passengers sit in cars called coaches. Most short-distance
commuter trains have only coach cars. Long-distance inter-city
trains offer passengers more services and luxuries. They include
dining or snack cars and sleeping cars.

This is a double-deck coach on an inter-city train. It seats up to 170 people. That is almost twice as many people as a regular coach can hold.

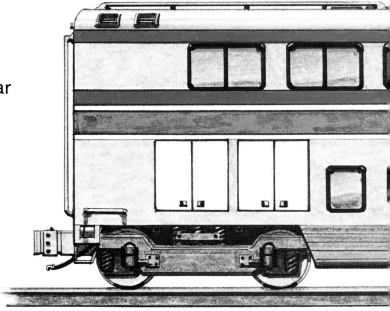

DOUBLE-DECK COACH

On an inter-city train, the coach has big reclining seats, arm rests, and plenty of leg room so the passengers will be comfortable during their long journey.

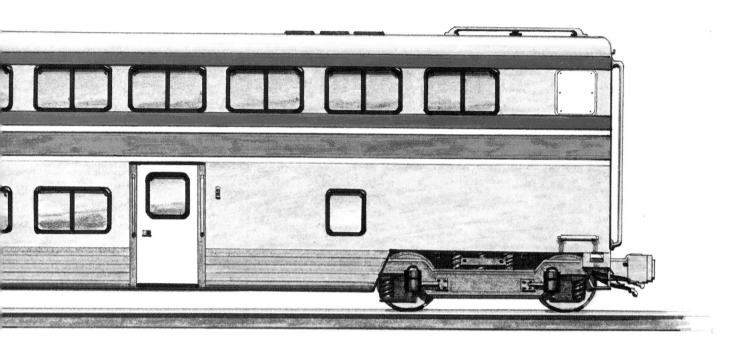

Some trains have an observation car. Here passengers relax and enjoy the view as the train speeds through the countryside.

The TGV trains in France have been nicknamed the "Oranges" because of their bright orange color. These special high-speed passenger trains can travel more than 200 miles per hour. They are some of the fastest trains in the world.

FRENCH TGV

The famous high-speed train in Japan is called the Shinkansen. It is nicknamed the "bullet train" because it appears to move like a speeding bullet when rushing by at speeds of more than 100 miles per hour. A Shinkansen train is almost totally automatic. Though it has an engineer, most of its operations are performed by remote control from a control center far away.

JAPANESE SHINKANSEN

SUBWAY TRAIN

Subway trains run on tracks in underground tunnels. Many big cities have subway systems. Sometimes the sidewalk rumbles as a subway train rushes through a tunnel underneath. Without subways, many city streets would be jammed with too many cars and buses.

Another way to avoid traffic jams on city streets is to build trains that travel on tracks above the street. These are called elevated trains, but they are usually called "els" for short. The tracks for an "el" train are held up by strong concrete beams.

ELEVATED TRAIN

MONORAIL

A monorail is an elevated train that travels on only one track, or rail. The rail runs either above or below the train. Many zoos and amusement parks use monorails to transport people from one area to another.

All through the day and night, trains criss-cross the country, carrying people and cargo to their destinations.